Introduction

MW01137321

Greetings! My name is Rene Davis and I am so glad that you have picked up my book, *The Sweet & Slim Dump Cake Cookbook: Your Easy Guide to Gluten-Free, Low Calorie, Low Sugar, and Low Fat Dump Cake Recipes.*

Inside this book, I have compiled my ultimate collection of my favorite dump cake recipes for you to bake! The reason that I personally love dump cakes is that they are very easy to prepare and bake as well as the fact that they are absolutely delicious! In this book, you'll find recipes anywhere from rhubarb strawberry to decadent chocolate!

All of these recipes have are easy to put together and bake. It's great news for any of you who are new to dump cakes!

This edition of my cookbook series features a health conscious theme. I believe that you should have your cake and eat it too! For those of you who have certain dietary restrictions, I understand how difficult it is to continuously watch what you are eating. Whether you're diabetic or celiac, there's something in this book for you! And for those who just want to look at healthier dessert options, you've come to the right place!

So, have at it! Dive into this book and learn more about the benefits of healthier dump cake alternative and start baking with ease!

Happy baking,

Rene Davis

Founder of Homegrown Publishing

-Your Personal Guide to Homemade Goods -

Table of Contents

About the Author

Rene Davis currently works a Public Relations Associate for a marketing firm in San Francisco, CA. She was born on February 22, 1988 to her parents Shawn and Lorie Davis in Eugene, Oregon.

She graduated Cum Laude from Oregon State University in 2009 with a degree in Strategic Communications and hopes to one day start her own sustainable food company.

She has a true appreciation and appetite for baked goods and fine dining, which stems from her grandmother who always told her, "Food is so essential to living a full life. Therefore, make it good and eat it often."

In her free time, Rene loves to ski, play with her Corgi named Benny, cook for her friends and sing in the shower when nobody is home.

What are Dump Cakes and How Can I Make Them?

Have you ever heard of what a dump cake is? Sounds like a pretty odd name for a dessert, right? However, I don't want to give anyone the wrong idea. Dump cakes are incredibly delicious desserts that are very easy to make.

The name says it all. You dump the ingredients into a pan and toss it into the oven. It's that simple! Most dump cakes require little to no preparation and nearly all the ingredients can be found at your local grocery store.

The directions for these recipes are generally simple. Most don't go further than 5-7 steps, but for some of the fancier recipes that require more steps, you'll be deservingly rewarded with a delicious dump cake nonetheless.

The Benefits of Low Calorie, Low Sugar, Low Fat, & Gluten Free Diets*

Low Calorie

In low-calorie diets, you usually are consuming between 800 and 1,500 calories. Some people use this diet for alternative short-term weight loss.

Losing weight during this diet may improve weight-related medical condition, including but not limited to diabetes, high cholesterol and high blood pressure. However, low calorie diets aren't more or less effective than your standard diet. As soon as you get off the diet, certain lifestyle changes, a commitment to healthy eating and regular physical activity are a must.

Talk to your dietician or doctor about your personal health needs and whether or not you'll be getting sufficient nutrients while on a low calorie diet.

Low Sugar

Drastically lowering your refined sugar intake or eliminating it completely from your diet can prove to be great for your health. When we talk about refined sugar, we're talking about the processed junk and not the naturally occurring sugars in fruits or veggies.

When trying a low sugar diet, your body may go through some withdrawals, which may include headaches, fatigue and excessive cravings for sugar. The best way to combat this is by drinking plenty of water and getting enough exercise.

As a result of adopting this low sugar lifestyle, you may experience some added bonuses to your health. Your sugar cravings may be reduced, you will have less "hunger pains", and improved focus and mental state, rapid weight loss, and overall increased general health.

Low Fat

A low-fat diet can have many advantages. The obvious weight loss is given, but there are more health benefits to lowering your daily fat intake.

By eating more foods that are filling and lower in fat, you can help ward off some serious medical conditions such as heart disease, high cholesterol and diabetes.

However, the body does need some fat to function properly. Not all fat is bad. For about every gram of fat are 9 calories. Some fats are better than others:

Unsaturated fats: (plant based, corn, canola oils, corn). These include monounsaturated and polyunsaturated fats. When you are on a low-fat diet, most of your fats would be coming from this category.

Saturated fats: (animal products, dairy, meat). These can increase your risk of heart disease if excessively consumed. "According to the National Institutes of Health (NIH) 10 percent of less of your daily calories should come from saturated fats. The American Heart Association recommends even less – 7 percent."

Gluten Free

More grocery stores these days are carrying gluten-free products. This is great for people living with celiac disease. However, most people who do make their way to gluten free products don't even have sensitivity to wheat or gluten. Many people just perceive gluten as being healthier.

Gluten-free means staying away from many common and nutritious foods. Gluten is a protein that is found in wheat, barley, and rye.

Going gluten-free as an individual living without celiac disease doesn't offer special nutritional benefits. Many whole grains that contain gluten are rich in an array of vitamins and minerals (e.g. B vitamins, iron, fiber)

Make the smart choice when you're searching for gluten-free products. Not all of the foods in the store that are marketed are healthy. Be cognizant about that.

*DISCLAIMER: I am not a medical doctor or dietician. The following researched reports on low calorie, low sugar, low fat

The Sweet & Slim Dump Cake Cookbook: The Ultimate Selection of Gluten Free, Low Calorie, Low Sugar, and Low Fat and Dump Cake Recipes

Easy-Peasy Fruit Festive Dump Cake

It doesn't get easier than this. These ingredients are incredibly easy to come by at your local grocery store. This is a great starter recipe for you and your family. You may use any assortment of fruit that you like. Whatever frozen fruit you can find around the house or maybe take a trip to the store and pick out your favorites! I personally love a berry mix with peaches. It's so easy, your kids will enjoy creating this dump cake with you! Or even better, they'll love the recipe so much they'll just make the dump cake for you!

INGREDIENTS:

3 cups of any assortment of frozen fruit

1 box of sugar free yellow or white cake mix

1 can of Sprite or 7-Up (you may use low calorie/diet)

DIRECTIONS:

Set oven at 350 degrees.

Place the frozen fruit into a 9" x 13" baking dish.

Pour the dry cake mix over the top of the fruit.

Pour the soda over the cake mix slowly and carefully. NOTE: Don't stir the mix. The cake mix will be the crust for this cake.

Bake at 350 degrees for 45 - 50 minutes.

Low-Calorie Cherry Pineapple Paradise Dump Cake

Love to keep your desserts low calorie and still to die for? Try out this easy to make recipe that includes delicious reduced calorie cherry pie filling and crushed pineapples! Can you say YUM! It's great for any occasion! Good for a party of up to 20 of your closest friends and family!

INGREDIENTS:

1 box of Super Moist Yellow Cake

1 can of Dole Crushed Pineapple in 100% Pineapple juice (20 oz)

1 can of Reduced Calorie Cherry Pie Filling (20 oz)

1/2 cup of light margarine (gluten free if preferred)

DIRECTIONS:

Set the oven to 350 degrees.

Take out 9" x 13" baking dish and spray it with non-stick spray.

Open the crushed pineapple and spread them on the baking dish evenly.

Use a spoon to lather the cherry filling on top of the pineapple.

Spread the dry cake mix over the fruit evenly.

Place dish into the oven and bake for 50 minutes or until golden crispy.

Cobbler Crazy Apple Dump Cake

This has got to be a fan favorite among apple lovers. The taste of this cake is fantastic and best of all, it is low calorie, easy to make, and will make your mouth explode with flavor! The preparation is so simple anyone can do it! Be prepared to have your sweet cravings fulfilled because this cake is going to take you on a journey to dump cake heaven!

INGREDIENTS:

½ box of Sugar-Free yellow cake mix

1 can of apple pie filling/any other fruit of your liking (no sugar

added)

4 tbsp of fat free butter, melted

½ tsp natural ground cinnamon

¼ tsp natural ground nutmeg

DIRECTIONS:

Set the oven to 350 degrees

Use a 9" x 13" baking dish and spray with nonstick spray

Pour the apple pie filling onto the dish as your first layer

Layer the top of the apple pie filling with the cinnamon and

nutmeg evenly

Pour the ½ box of sugar free on top of the fruit filling

Evenly pour the melted butter over the entire dish

If you wish, use a spoon to mix the fruit and cake mix and melted butter

Place the dish in the oven. For a "gooey-er" taste bake for 25 minutes. For a crispier taste bake for 45-50 minutes.

Gluten-Free Apple Pear Paradise Dump Cake

The pear and the apple are like long lost siblings, right? I don't often put the two together because they're often good by themselves. However, when they are put together in a delicious dish like this, I can't refuse to eat them both together! Try this recipe out and let it take your to paradise!

INGREDIENTS

1 box of gluten free yellow cake mix

1 large can of pears w/ juice (sliced)

1 jar of chunky applesauce (or apple pie filling)

1-¼ sticks of butter

¼ cup of organic brown sugar

DIRECTIONS

Set the oven to 350 degrees

Spray an 9" x 13" baking dish with nonstick spray

Spread the chunky applesauce on the bottom layer of the baking dish

Sprinkle the brown sugar on top (note: if you use apple pie filling, don't use brown sugar

Take the pears and cut them into small pieces and place those on top.

Pour the juice gently over the top. Do not mix.

Pour the cake mix on top pear layer.

Slice the butter into ¼" pats and spread on top of the cake mix evenly.

Take the dish and place in the oven. Bake for 50 minutes or until golden.

Light and Sweet Fruit Lover's Dump Cake

Another easy recipe for fruit lovers! Take any assortment of your favorite frozen fruits and soda! It's so simple it's a piece of cake! (Pun intended). Let this recipe dazzle your friends and family. Or perhaps you'd like to share this recipe with your lover! They will thank you for it and will want to try the recipe themselves.

INGREDIENTS

Frozen fruit of any assortment (strawberries, peaches, cherries, blueberries, etc.)

1 box of sugar free yellow cake mix

1 can of soda (Sprite or any cream soda)

¼ cup of chopped walnuts, almonds, or peanuts

DIRECTIONS

Set the oven to 350 degrees

Spray an 8" x 8" baking dish with nonstick spray

Take the frozen fruit and place evenly on the baking dish

Sprinkle the cake mix on top of the fruit

Evenly pour the soda on top of the mix.

Sprinkle the top layer with the chopped nuts. (DO NOT STIR)

Place the dish in the oven and bake for 40-45 minutes.

Low-Fat Fruit Festive Dump Cake

Your family will absolutely love this dish. It is going to go fast at family gatherings. This dump cake recipe does not call for any extra sweeteners or additives, so this will be a lower fat version of the traditional dump cake. Honestly, your loved ones wouldn't be able to tell the difference.

INGREDIENTS

3 cups of your choice of fruit

1 box (16 Oz. Size) Angel Food Cake Mix

1 cup of water

DIRECTIONS

Set the oven to 350 degrees

Use a 9" x 13" baking dish

Spray the baking dish with a non-stick spray.

Place your choice of fruit as the base layer of the dish. Spread evenly.

Use the cake mix to cover the fruit layer evenly. You don't have to use the entire box if you're making a smaller dish.

Use the water to cover the layer of dry cake mix. Only use enough to ensure full coverage over the mix.

Optional: sprinkle the top with nutmeg or cinnamon.

Place the dish in the preheated oven and bake for 35-45 minutes (depending on the size of your dish)

Fit-Friendly Berry Cobbler Dump Cake

For those of you who have that craving for sweets after the gym because you think you deserve it, you no longer have to feel guilty with this recipe! Dieting does not have to be a punishment. You want to be kind to yourself and treat yourself once in a while with a nice, guilt free treat. This Berry Cobbler is just for you! It's easy and delicious and less than 150 calories!

INGREDIENTS

1 box of moist cake mix (vanilla gluten free/low calorie preferred)

1 can of diet soda (Sprite)

24 oz of frozen mixed berries

DIRECTIONS

Heat the oven to 350 degrees

Use a 9" x 13" baking dish and cover with nonstick spray

Cover the bottom layer evenly with your frozen fruit

Place the dry cake mix on top of the fruit

Slowly pour the soda over the top. DO NOT MIX. This will give the crusty top

Place the dish in the oven and bake for 45-50 minutes.

Berry Oh' Berry Light Dump Cake

Berries on berries on berries! Well, blueberries and blackberries that is. Everyone loves berries, right? I know I do. This one is so refreshing and so crisp. Oh, and did I mention, light! That's all I can really say about berries. They're just so good for you! Try this recipe out! I know you'll like it!

INGREDIENTS

3 ½ cups of fresh blueberries

3 ½ cups of fresh blackberries

¼ cup of powdered sugar

1 tsp of ground cinnamon

1 box of gluten free yellow cake mix

6 tbsp of fat-free sour cream

½ cup of fat-free half-and-half

1 tsp butter extract (optional)

DIRECTIONS

Heat the oven to 350 degrees

Use a 9" x 13" baking dish and cover with nonstick spray

Put the blackberries, blueberries, and powdered sugar all together in a large bowl. Then spoon that evenly into the baking dish.

Take the cake mix and cover the fruit evenly.

In a bowl, mix together the fat-free sour cream, fat free half-and-half and butter extract (if you wish) in a blender or food processor until it is smooth. Pour that smooth mix on top of the cake mix.

Place the baking dish in the oven and bake for 40 minutes or until golden brown. Serve warm or cold. Enjoy!

Reduced-Fat Pumpkin Prestige Dump Cake

A great recipe for you pumpkin lovers out there! This recipe uses real pumpkin instead of the pie fillings that come from a can. Also, using pumpkin-pie spice instead of just cinnamon can be a great choice for the optimal flavoring of your cake. You can bring this recipe to life during the fall season to dazzle your friends and family! It's an incredibly special dessert.

INGREDIENTS

1 can of pumpkin (29 oz)

2 eggs

1 egg white

1 can of evaporated skim milk (12 oz)

¾ cup sugar

2 teaspoons pumpkin-pie spice

1 box yellow cake mix

¼ cup melted butter

2/3-cup low fat buttermilk

1/3 cup pecans, chopped

DIRECTIONS

Set the oven to 350 degrees

Use a 9" x 13" pan and spray it with nonstick cooking spray

Using a large enough bowl, take the pumpkin, evaporated milk, eggs, sugar and pumpkin-pie spice and whisk them together. Pour the mix into the baking pan.

Spread the cake mix over the top of the first layer. Add the buttermilk and butter and pour that on top of the cake mix. Add pecans on top.

Take the pan and place it in the oven and let it bake for 45-50 minutes.

Low-Sugar Cherry Champion Dump Cake

This is another variation of the dump cake that families will love. This one has added shredded coconuts and chopped pecans. Low sugar is always great! Have this one ready for your loved ones! They'll truly appreciate this dump cake. It's a dump cake truly made for a champion!

INGREDIENTS

1 can of crushed pineapple

1 can of cherry pie filling (no sugar added)

1 stick of gluten free butter (or low fat)

1 cup of shredded coconut

1 cup of chopped pecans

DIRECTIONS

Set the oven for 350 degrees

Use a 9" x 13" baking pan.

Spray the baking pan with nonstick spray.

Spread the can of cherry pie filling and pineapple to the bottom layer of the baking pan (NOTE: do not drain) Mix thoroughly.

Spread coconut over the top

Spread the cake mix evenly over the coconut

Top off the entire thing with chopped pecans evenly

Place the pan in the oven and bake for 35-40 minutes.

Nana's Nearly Sugar-Free Apple Dump Cake

Who doesn't love sugar free recipes? Who doesn't love apples? This recipe is simply delicious. If you have a love for having mouth-gasms, this dump cake will surely satisfy you. It will be an explosion of flavor in your mouth! Your grandmother would surely be proud.

INGREDIENTS

1 box of Yellow Cake Mix (sugar free)

2 cans of apple pie filling (no sugar added)

½ tsp of nutmeg

¼ tsp of ginger

1 tsp of cinnamon

1 cup of melted butter (low fat)

DIRECTIONS:

Set the oven to 350 degrees

Use a 9" x "13 baking pan and evenly grease it up with nonstick spray

Spread evenly the 2 cans of apple pie filling on the bottom of the pan

Using a separate bowl, mix together the cake mix, cinnamon, nutmeg, and ginger.

In another bowl, melt the butter in the microwave.

Evenly spread the cake mix over the top of the apple pie filling

Evenly pour the melted butter on top of the cake mix

Take the pan; place it in the oven and bake for 35-40 minutes until the top is slightly golden brown

Have the dump cake sit for about an hour before serving. Enjoy!

Gluten-Free Blueberry Bonanza Dump Cake

Blueberries! Blueberries! Blueberries! This delicious dish is gluten free and is incredible appealing to you hungry health conscious folk! Have no fear, individuals living with celiac sprue. This cake will taste amazing. You'll be happy you had it!

INGREDIENTS

1 large can of crushed pineapple (including juice)

1 large can of blueberry pie filling, no high fructose corn or syrup/additives/dyes

1 box of gluten-free yellow cake mix

1 stick of unsalted butter or margarine

1 cup of chopped nuts (optional)

1 cup of coconut shavings (optional)

DIRECTIONS

Set the oven to 350 degrees

Use a 9" x "13 baking pan and evenly grease it up with nonstick spray. Sprinkle a tiny bit of the cake mix on the bottom on the pan.

Dump the crushed pineapple on the bottom layer of the baking pan evenly.

Dump the blueberry pie filling on top of the pineapple evenly.

Dump the gluten free- yellow cake mix on top of the pineapple evenly.

Heat the butter so it melts. Pour on top of the entire dry cake mix.

If you wish, add the chopped nuts and coconut shavings to the top of the entire dish.

Place the dish in the oven and bake for 50-60 minutes.

Take the dish out of the oven and let it cool.

Enjoy with or without a creamy topping!

Blueberry Blitz Cream Cheese Dump Cake

Who feels guilty after they eat a slice of cheesecake? I know I do. If you want something a bit lighter but still have the deliciousness and flavor as a cheesecake, try this Blueberry Cream Cheese Delight Dump Cake Recipe! You'll absolutely love it!

INGREDIENTS

20 oz can of blueberry pie filling

8 oz block of cream cheese

16 oz box of yellow cake mix (low sugar preferred)

4 oz stick of margarine, partially frozen

Cooking oil spray

DIRECTIONS

Set the oven to 350 degrees

Use a 9" x "13 baking pan and evenly grease it up with nonstick spray. Sprinkle a tiny bit of the cake mix on the bottom on the pan.

Pour the blueberry pie filling into the pan and spread evenly.

Slice the cream cheese into cubes and spread evenly over the filling. (best if chilled)

Sprinkle the cake mix evenly over the pie filling.

Slice the margarine into thin slices. It's best if the margarine is partially frozen.

Place the margarine slices evenly on top of the cake mix.

Place in the oven. Bake 40-45 minutes.

Pumpkin Pecan Pleasure Dump Cake

The ultimate fall season dump cake recipe. With a little bit of pumpkin, a little bit of pecan, and little bit of spice and whole lot of pleasure for those seeking a great dessert! An incredible dessert to bring to any family gathering! Better bring enough because this cake is gonna go fast!

INGREDIENTS

1 can (30 oz.) pumpkin pie filling

1 box butter cake mix (low sugar preferred)

2 cans (12 oz.) evaporated milk

1 cup of light brown sugar

6 large eggs

1 cup of butter, (fat free preferred)

2 cups of chopped pecans

½ cup granulated sugar

1 tbsp. ground cinnamon

DIRECTIONS

Set the oven to 350 degrees

Use a 9" x "13 baking pan and evenly grease it up with nonstick spray. Sprinkle a tiny bit of the cake mix on the bottom on the pan.

Using a large bowl, take the pumpkin, evaporated milk, brown sugar and eggs and mix them well together until smooth.

Add in ONLY 1 cup chopped pecans to the bowl

Pour the mix from the bowl into the pan and spread the cake mix evenly on top

Use the remaining pecans and sprinkle that on top.

Take the melted butter and pour it on top of the entire dish.

Combine the granulated sugar and cinnamon and sprinkle it on top of the cake

Place the pan in the oven and bake for 1 hour and 10 minutes.

Take the pan out and let it sit for 10 minutes so the center can set.

Gluten-Free Pineapple Cherry Dump Cake

The gluten free version of a summertime favorite! It's incredibly easy to make, you won't even beat a sweat. This is a great time to have your kids help out with the preparation! Some similar recipes call for more butter, but this one is just enough to satisfy any extra cravings for a rich dessert.

INGREDIENTS:

1 box of yellow cake mix (gluten free, try Betty Crocker)

1 can of (20oz) Crushed Pineapple

2 cans of (15oz) Dark Sweet Cherries, no high fructose corn or syrup/additives/dyes, (drained)

1 stick of unsalted butter (sliced into 1/4 inch pats)

DIRECTIONS

Set the oven to 350 degrees.

Take out 9" x 13" baking dish and spray it with non-stick spray.

Open the crushed pineapple and spread them on the baking dish evenly.

Use a spoon to lather the cherry filling (without the juice) on top of the pineapple evenly. (add juice to find the right consistency of your liking and mix)

Spread the dry cake mix over the fruit evenly.

Place the butter pats evenly on top of the cake mix.

Place dish into the oven and bake for 50-60 minutes or until golden crispy

Peach Lover's Healthy Gluten-Free Dump Cake

What is your favorite summer fruit? I know what mine is and it's definitely included in this Peach Lover's Healthy Gluten Free Dump Cake. This one calls for a few more ingredients than the other recipes, but you'll be drooling over this cake when it's finished. Definitely put some whipped topping or ice cream on top if you wish. That's what I love to do and my friends and family love it as well!

DIRECTIONS

3 large peaches, diced

½ box of vanilla gluten-free cake mix

¾ cup of unsweetened applesauce, divided

1 cup of fat-free evaporated milk, divided

2 tbsp of coconut oil, melted

1 tsp. cinnamon, divided

DIRECTIONS

Set the oven to 350 degrees.

Take out 8" x 8" baking dish and spray it with non-stick spray.

Put the diced peaches on the baking pan evenly.

Spoon ½ cup of the applesauce on top of the peaches followed by ½ cup of the evaporated milk. Then, dollop ½ tsp of the cinnamon on top.

Evenly sprinkle the cake mix on top of the peaches.

Dollop the remaining applesauce and evaporated milk on top of the cake mix.

Sprinkle the remaining cinnamon.

Drizzle the coconut oil on top of the cake and use a spatula to carefully spread all of the ingredients on top. Be sure that the dry cake mix is not exposed.

Take the baking pan and place it in the oven. Bake for 35-45 minutes or until golden crispy and bubbling.

Remove from oven. Let it cool before serving. Enjoy!

Gluten-Free Peach Pleasure Cobbler Dump Cake

This is a recipe that everyone will love. It's all about the peaches and you don't want to miss this. Sometimes gluten free cake mixes don't turn out the way you planned with other fruits or recipes, but this one is a definite winner compared the original peach cobbler.

INGREDIENTS

1 can sliced peaches (20oz) with the juice

1 gluten free yellow cake mix

½ cup of butter (melted)

1 cup of nuts of your choosing (chopped)

DIRECTIONS

Set the oven to 350 degrees.

Take out a 9" x 13" baking dish and spray it with non-stick spray.

Pour the peaches into the baking pan.

Spread the dry cake mix over the peaches.

Spoon the melted butter over the top of the cake mix evenly.

Take the nuts and sprinkle them on top.

Place the baking dish into the oven and bake for 45-50 minutes. Serve cold or warm.

Banana Mango Mantra Dump Cake

Feeling up for a little "peace" of paradise with this tropical inspired dump cake recipe? Sit on the beach with the toes in the sand! This is exactly what the Banana Mango Mantra Dump Cake recipe does; it brings you to a delicious paradise.

INGREDIENTS

2 cups of mangos (I prefer the softer kind)

2 ripe bananas (thin slices)

1 box of gluten-free yellow cake mix (vanilla)

1 stick of unsalted butter or margarine

1 cup of coconut shavings (optional)

DIRECTIONS

Set the oven to 350 degrees

Use a 9" x "13 baking pan and evenly grease it up with nonstick spray. Sprinkle a tiny bit of the cake mix on the bottom on the pan.

Dump the sliced mangos on the bottom layer of the baking pan evenly.

Dump the sliced bananas on top of the pineapple evenly.

Dump the gluten-free yellow cake mix on top of the fruit evenly.

Heat the butter so it melts. Pour on top of the entire dry cake mix.

If you wish, add the coconut shavings to the top of the entire dish.

Place the dish in the oven and bake for 45-55 minutes or until golden brown.

Take the dish out of the oven and let it cool.

Enjoy with or without a creamy topping! Welcome to paradise!

Chocolate Charm Dump Cake

This is rich and delicious dessert that you and your loved ones will absolutely enjoy! Who doesn't love chocolate, that's the question. Be sure to share this recipe with everyone you know! It's to die for!

INGREDIENTS

1 cup of flour (or Gluten Free)

2 tsp baking powder

3 tbsp margarine (melted)

¾ cup of sugar / ½ cup of sugar

½ cup of brown sugar

3 tbsp of cocoa / ¼ cup of cocoa (separate)

½ cup of almond milk

1/2 tsp vanilla extract

1 1/2 cup water

DIRECTIONS

Set the oven to 350 degrees.

Take out an 8" x 8" baking dish and spray it with non-stick spray.

Using a large bowl, combine the flour, ¾ cup of sugar and baking powder.

Melt the margarine and combine that with 3 tbsp of cocoa in a mixing cup. Add this to the dry ingredients.

Beat together the almond milk and vanilla extract. Pour into the baking dish.

Sprinkle the brown sugar, ½ cup of sugar, and ¼ cup of cocoa on top. Don't mix.

Carefully pour the water on top.

Place the baking dish in the oven and bake for 40-45 minutes.

Serve hot or cold, with or without a topping of your choice.

Gluten Free Chocolate Cherry Dump Cake

Does gluten free, chocolate, and cherries go together? That's an absolute yes! Nothing sounds more alluring than cherries and chocolate. It's the ultimate mix between health conscious and rich tasting. It's absolutely going to rock your world! You may even want to serve this one with whipped cream or ice cream on top! It's up to you! Your taste buds will thank you.

INGREDIENTS

1 can of cherry pie filling (27oz), no high fructose corn or syrup/additives/dyes

1 box of gluten free chocolate cake mix

1 cup of unsalted butter

1 cup of crushed almonds (or any nuts of your liking)

DIRECTIONS

Set the oven to 350 degrees.

Take out a 9" x 13" baking dish and spray it with non-stick spray.

Evenly pour the cherry pie filling into the baking dish.

Pour the chocolate cake mix over the top of the cherries evenly.

Cut the butter into ¼ inch slices and evenly distribute on top of the cake mix.

Place the crushed almonds (or any nuts of your liking) on top.

Place the baking dish into the oven and bake for 50-60 minutes.

Strawberry Summer Rhubarb Dump Cake

I absolutely love this dessert! It's a new favorite of mine and I'm just going to keep making it over and over again for my friends, my family and myself! Together, strawberries and rhubarb go together like a perfect couple. This cake will not leave you feeling guilty at all. You will love it! Your kids will love it! Your spouse will love it! Don't waste any more time. This one is a winner!

INGREDIENTS

6 cups of rhubarb (sliced into 1" pieces)

2 cups of water

2 pints of strawberries (chopped)

1 box of gluten-free Yellow Cake Mix

¾ cup of vegan butter

DIRECTIONS

Set the oven to 350 degrees.

Take out a 9" x 13" baking dish and spray it with non-stick spray.

Take the chopped rhubarb and sauté it in a pan with the 2 cups of water for 5 minutes, or until it is slightly soft.

Add the rhubarb with the juice to the chopped strawberries. Mix well.

Put the fruit into the baking dish.

Take the cake mix and sprinkle on top of the fruit.

Melt the butter in a microwave or stovetop and spread evenly on top of the cake mix.

Place the baking dish into the oven and bake for 35-45 minutes or until golden brown. Once finished, take it out of the oven and let it cool for 10 minutes.

Serve with or without your favorite topping! Enjoy.

Heavenly Honey Gluten-Free Dump Cake

This is a true classic, but now with a gluten-free, lower fat twist! I can't fully express how much I love this recipe. It tastes really great with any of your favorite fruit, but I personally love it with cherry and pineapple. Blueberry works great with this one as well! It tastes amazing either hot or cold, with or without a creamy topping or ice cream! You can get the polenta at any health foods store! Get to it! You won't regret it!

INGREDIENTS

1 can pineapple chunks (20oz), drained

1 can cherry pie filling (21oz)

1 package plain-flavored prepared polenta (18oz), cut into chunks

¼ cup honey (raw, thick works best)

1/8 cup plain yogurt

½ tsp ground cinnamon

1/8 tsp ground cardamom

3 tbsp salted butter, softened

DIRECTIONS

Set the oven to 350 degrees.

Take out a 9" x 9" baking dish and spray it with non-stick spray.

Pour the drained pineapple chunks onto the baking dish and then spread the cherry pie filling on top.

Take the chunks of polenta along with the honey and yogurt and put them into a food processor or blender and mix until fully blended.

Now add the cinnamon and cardamom to the polenta mix and process until fully blended.

Add the softened butter to the polenta mixture and process the mixture once more until well blended.

Pour the polenta mixture over the top of the cherry-pineapple mixture.

Take the baking dish and place it in the oven. Bake for 40 minutes on the center rack.

Remove from the oven and let it cool for 10 minutes. Enjoy!

Made in the USA
Lexington, KY
23 September 2014